THE P[...]

EDWAR[...]

Books by Liz Shakespeare

The Memory Be Green:
An Oral History of a Devon Village

~

Fever: A Story from a Devon Churchyard

~

The Turning of the Tide

~

All Around The Year

~

The Postman Poet

For details go to www.lizshakespeare.co.uk

THE POEMS OF EDWARD CAPERN

Selected by
Liz Shakespeare

LETTERBOX BOOKS

This selection published 2017
by
Letterbox Books
Littleham
Bideford
Devon
EX39 5HW

www.lizshakespeare.co.uk

ISBN 978-0-9516879-5-6

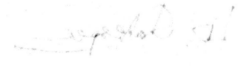

Printed and bound by SRP Ltd, Exeter

CONTENTS

Introduction by Liz Shakespeare

INTRODUCTION

Edward Capern (1819 – 1894) is known as the Devonshire Postman Poet. His poems celebrate the North Devon countryside through which he walked on his postman's round, giving us a vivid picture of lanes resplendent with flowers and birdsong; they tell stories of the people he met as he delivered the Penny Post and they demand social justice for the poor.

Despite his humble occupation and lack of formal education, he received national recognition and was able to count Charles Dickens, Charles Kingsley, Baroness Burdett-Coutts and the poet Walter Savage Landor amongst his supporters. He received many visitors who arrived in Bideford by the newly opened railway, keen to see the scenes described by the postman poet.

Four volumes of poems and one book of songs were published to national acclaim and most ran to second or third editions. He was referred to as 'the Devonshire Burns'. He gave talks and readings throughout England; his songs were sung around pianos in drawing rooms and his poems learnt by heart in schools. His name is still known by many in North Devon and articles are written about him from time to time, but few people today have read Edward Capern's poems.

It is time for a revival of interest.

Edward Capern was born in Tiverton in 1819, the eldest son of a baker. The family moved to Barnstaple when he was very young, following in the footsteps of lace workers who moved there from Tiverton to work in the new lace factory. The family were poor; from the age of nine he was forced to work very long hours in the lace factory to help support his siblings. He later tried a variety of occupations including shoemaker, carpenter, French polisher and even portrait painter but it would appear that he was not very successful at any of them. It was eight years after meeting his future wife, Jane Trick, that they were finally able to marry and settle in Bideford.

Edward had attended school for only four months, but had quickly learnt to read. There were no free libraries at this time and the family would have been unable to buy books, but salvation came when the Literary and Scientific Institution was opened in Barnstaple in 1845 and Edward was offered free membership, which included access to its extensive library, by its founder and benefactor, William Frederick Rock.

Rock was the son of a Barnstaple shoemaker. He founded a successful printing company in London and, having no wife or children, gave generously to his home town. He took an active interest in Edward Capern's progress and they corresponded throughout their lives. Following the publication of Capern's early poems in the *North Devon Journal*, Rock used his influence to enable the first book of poems to be published, the list of subscribers including the Prime Minister, Lord Tennyson, Charles Dickens, many members of the aristocracy and, of course, Capern's numerous supporters in North Devon.

The book was a resounding success, receiving positive reviews in newspapers throughout England which resulted in the first edition of a thousand copies selling out in a matter of weeks. The Prime Minister was so impressed by the patriotic poem *The Lion Flag of England* that he sent broadsheet copies to soldiers serving in the Crimea, and awarded Capern a Civil List Pension of £40 a year – considerably more than he received in wages from the Post Office.

He continued with his postal round from Bideford to Buckland Brewer, composing poems as he walked and writing them down at the kitchen table of a cottage where he spent a few hours before walking back to Bideford with the return post. His second book *Ballads and Songs* followed in 1858; *The Devonshire Melodist*, a book of songs, in 1861; *Wayside Warbles* in 1865 with a greatly expanded edition in 1870; and *Sungleams and Shadows* in 1881.

Capern's rural poetry, celebrating the countryside in all its moods throughout the seasons, held attractions for readers living in an increasingly urbanised and industrialised country. Much of his verse depicts an idealised world and, in common with most literature of the time, does not challenge the accepted status quo of 'the rich man in his castle, the poor man at his gate.' William Rock would have advised him that his poetry could not be published if he offended those in positions of authority. However, Capern was outspoken at times in his demands for the rich to support the poor, most notably in *The Old Stone-Breaker*, and frequently slipped in reminders of the destitute amongst his happier lyrics. Rock's advice was sound; Capern was one of very few working-class writers whose work found favour with Downing Street and who eventually achieved financial independence through writing.

His life story is remarkable. It is the subject of my novel *The Postman Poet* and also a biography by his great-great-granddaughter, Ilfra Goldberg, published in 2009 but sadly out of print at the time of writing this introduction. It is perhaps due to the perceived romance of an impoverished postman writing poems as he walked that the name of Edward Capern is still remembered, but the few people who attempt to read his poems today, perhaps by seeking them out in the reference section of the local library, tend to be overwhelmed by the sheer number of poems – close to six hundred between the four volumes.

Poems that were praised at the time of publication for their cheerfulness and innocence can appear naïve and over-romanticised in today's more cynical times. There are technical weaknesses in some poems and others are derivative. *The Seagull* for example, praised by Charles Kingsley, is heavily influenced by James Hogg's *The Lark*.

However, the best poems are as fresh and natural today as they were a hundred and fifty years ago and have an authenticity which reaches down to us through the years, creating a picture of simple rural life in the lanes and hamlets of North Devon. The music of the countryside and the rhythm of the postman's footsteps can be detected in the cadence of the verses. His voice has a genuine, warm humanity and spontaneity of feeling which eloquently communicates both the pleasure he takes in nature, as in poems such as *A Maytime Wish,* and the sadness of *Under the Snow,* a poem which would be intensely moving even if one did not know of the family tragedy that brought it into being.

Some of Edward Capern's poems were intended to be sung. The songs had been largely forgotten because, naturally, no recordings could be made at the time, but they can now be heard again on the C.D. *The Songs of Edward Capern* recorded by

Nick Wyke and Becki Driscoll (www.englishfiddle.com) and launched alongside my two books.

I have not included the lyrics of the recorded songs within this selection but there have, nevertheless, been hard decisions to make while attempting to whittle down the poems to a number which will please but not overwhelm the modern reader. I have chosen those which I consider to have the greatest poetic merit, but have also included poems which I feel to be of particular interest in relation to Edward Capern himself, and to the locality.

Edward Capern deserves a larger audience. I hope this selection brings enjoyment to many people.

Liz Shakespeare ~ 2017

In recognition of Edward Capern's commitment to social justice, £1 from each copy sold will be donated to the Northern Devon Food Bank, charity no. 1162651.

from THE RURAL POSTMAN

, the postman's is as pleasant a life

As any one's, I trow;
For day by day he wendeth his way,
Where a thousand wildlings grow.
He marketh the date of the snowdrop's birth,
And knows when the time is near
For white scented violets to gladden the earth,
And sweet primrose groups t' appear.
He can show you the spot where the hyacinth wild
Hangs out her bell blossoms o' blue;
And tell where the celandine's bright-eyed child
Fills her chalice with honey dew.
The purple-dyed violet, the hawthorn and sloe,
The creepers that trail in the lane,
The dragon, the daisy, and clover-rose, too,
And buttercups gilding the plain;
The foxglove, the robert, the gorse, and the thyme,
The heather and broom on the moor,
And the sweet honeysuckle that loveth to climb
The arch of the cottager's door.
He knoweth them all, and he loveth them well,
And others not honoured with fame,
For they hang round his life like a beautiful spell,

And light up his path with their flame.
O, a pleasant life is the postman's life
And a fine cheerful soul is he,
For he'll shout and sing like a forest king,
On the crown of an ancient tree.
Heigho! I come and go,
Where the Lent lily, speedwell, and dog-rose blow,
Heigho! and merry, O!
Where hawkweeds, and trefoils, and wild peas grow.
Heigho! Heigho!
As pleasant as May-time, and light as a roe.

O, the postman's is as happy a life
As any one's, I trow;
Wand'ring away where dragon-flies play,
And brooks sing soft and slow;
And watching the lark as he soars on high,
To carol in yonder cloud,
"He sings in his labour, and why not I?"
The postman sings aloud.
And many a brace of humble rhymes
His pleasant soul hath made,
Of birds, and flowers, and happy times,
In sunshine and in shade.
The harvester, smiling, sees him pass,
"How goes the war?" quoth he;

And he stayeth his scythe in the corn or grass,
To learn what the news may be.
He honours the good, both rich and poor,
And jokes with each rosy-faced maid;
He nods at the aged dame at the door,
And patteth each urchin's head.
And little he thinks as he whistling goes,
To the march of some popular tune,
That beauty grows pale at the tramp of his shoes,
And sometimes as rosy as June.
O, a happy lad is the rural post,
And a right loyal servant, I ween;
For let a proud foe but threaten a blow,
He shouteth "Hurrah for the Queen!"
Heigho! I come and go,
Where the mountain ash and the alder grow.
Heigho! I come and go,
With a smile on my cheeks and a ruddy glow.

O, the postman's is as merry a life
As any one's, I trow;
Waking the hill with his musical trill,
From its crown to the base below.
For he windeth his horn where the blushing morn
First kisseth the green earth wide,
And snuffeth the breeze where the nodding trees

Stand strong in their forest pride.
He heareth the bee in the broad oak tree,
In quest of its honey-clad leaves,
And marks with delight when swallows alight
To build 'neath the cottager's eaves.
When forest tribes sing till green valleys ring
With the soul-stirring music they make,
His spirit as free as the fetterless sea,
Chants out o'er the meadow and brake.
When making his call at a nobleman's hall,
In garments bespattered and rude,
He thinks that sound health is the best of all wealth,
With a spirit in love with the good.
Full many a heart with a paper-winged dart,
Hath he wounded in Cupid's employ;
And trumpet-tongued Fame says that Hymen's bright
flame
Is fed by the honest old boy.
I'm welcome, he singeth, whenever I go,
When buds or bright blossoms appear,
At autumn-tide too, when golden tints glow,
And *most* when old Christmas is near.
Heigho! I come and go,
With the black seal of DEATH, and young LOVE's bow;
Heigho! I come and go,
With a smile for each joy, and a tear for each woe.

4

O, the postman's is as blessed a life
    As any one's, I trow,
If leaping the stile, o'er many a mile,
    Can blessedness bestow.
If tearing your way through a tangled wood,
    Or dragging your limbs through a lawn,—
If wading knee-deep through an angry flood,
    Or a ploughed field newly sown,—
If sweating big drops 'neath a burning sun,
    And shiv'ring 'mid sleet and snow;
If drenched to the skin with rain, be fun,
    And can a joy bestow!

from TO MILLY

Like summer, soft and breezy,
When swallows skim the sea,
Comes my song in numbers easy
And refreshing unto me.

So I'll pipe a lay to Milly,
The merry-making thing —
My pretty cottage lily,
And picture of the spring.

Oh, a beauty bright and brisky,
And musical as May,
Is my lassy, fair and frisky,
My little dancing fay.

In Nature's own adorning
This cherub thing appears,
And welcome as the morning
Is this pledge of loving years.

Like a starry glory dancing
In the cloudless ebon sky,
Is the wild romantic glancing
Of her laughter-lighted eye.

6

Would you see this pretty creature
In her wild and merry joy,
With a smile on every feature?
You must see her with my boy.

You must hear her accents choral,
Like the tones of silver rills,
As they gush from hedgerows floral,
To tinkle down the hills.

You have seen the lamb revealing
All its happy life could show,
While, with true maternal feeling,
Its dam would gambol too.

Not half so sweet and winning
Is that pretty scene to me,
As my little one's beginning
Her romp upon my knee.

Farewell to woodlands mossy,
And violets of the glade,
To daisies white and glossy,
And warblers of the shade.

Nor tell me of the lily,
Ye poets of the flowers,
Nor rose, while I have Milly
To beautify my hours.

AFFECTION'S ARGUMENT

The aspen quivers in the breeze,
The cuckoo singeth mellow;
The perfume drops from hawthorn trees —
Let's roam where the king-cup's yellow.
We'll cradle up our infant child,
And take our evening's ramble,
Adown the paths of woodland wild,
Through briar, thorn, and bramble.
I know in thy maternal breast
There dwells a sense of duty,
More lovely than the crimson west,
That robes the sun in beauty;
But still, I know, there is a charm
Reigns o'er each scene enchanting,
When we together, arm in arm,
Its beauties are descanting.
So toil not, gentle labourer,
I pray thee, toil not so;
Let's wander where the fragrant air
Doth health and joy bestow:
Or else I fear thy rosy cheek
Soon pale in death will be;

And then, alas! where could I seek
The bliss I find with thee ?

What boots it if we win this earth,
By striving and by toiling,
If we to dire disease give birth,
And cherish health's despoiling?
So leave, my love, this pent-up spot,
Thy every fear detaching;
Angels will hover o'er its cot,
The babe benignly watching;
And let us up some shady lane,
All torrent-washed and wearing,
To watch the pale moon's silver wane,
And take a gentle airing.
The antlered oak, the fretted thorn,
Thee to their nooks are wooing;
Whilst songs are on the breezes borne,
And turtle-doves are cooing.
So toil not, gentle labourer,
I pray thee, toil not so;
Let's wander where the fragrant air
Doth health and joy bestow:
Or else I fear thy rosy cheek
Soon pale in death will be;

And then, alas! where could I seek
The bliss I find with thee ?

I often think upon those times
When, blithesome, young, and smiling,
We listened to the bells' sweet chimes,
Our every care beguiling.
Then underneath some tree's broad shade
We sat and made us merry;
And never dreamt those joys would fade,
As melts the damask cherry.
But I have had since then to roam
Alone to take my pleasure;
And leave thee, dearest love, at home —
My sweetest, fondest treasure.
Come, let us to those fields again,
Each habit wrong subduing:
Such pleasures must be felt by twain,
And they are worth renewing.
So toil not, gentle labourer,
I pray thee, toil not so;
Let's wander where the fragrant air
Doth health and joy bestow:
Or else I fear thy rosy cheek
Soon pale in death will be;

And then, alas! where could I seek
The bliss I find with thee?

THE SEA-GULL

Bird of the ocean,
Graceful in motion,
Swift in thy passage from inland to sea;
Oft I in fancy pace
Over thy dwelling-place,
Dear to thy nestlings and precious to me.

Bright in eccentric flight,
Gleaming with purest white,
Floating through ether, all buoyant and free;
Raptured, I've seen thee swerve
From thy fantastic curve,
Dropping with call-note to sport on the lea.

Oft when the billows foam,
Far from thy native home,
Sheltered by woodland, near meadow and brook,
Over a rugged stile,
Thoughtful, I've leaned awhile,
Watching thee play with some blackamoor rook.

And on the shore I've stood,
Marking thy snowy brood

Dive 'neath the silver wave, searching for prey;
Then to the surface rise,
Soar to the fleecy skies,
Coo to thy comrades, and hasten away.

Bird of the ocean,
Graceful in motion,
Had I the pinions of Genius to soar,
Wild as thy airy flight,
I'd on her wings of light
All the fair regions of Fancy explore.

MY THOUGHTS

 ough stones from Nature's rudest bed,
Not shaped like those on beaches laid;
Unwashed by any classic surf,
They still retain their native turf.

THE RURAL POSTMAN'S SABBATH

The mellowed sounds of Sabbath bells
        Fall gently on my ear,
And as they break in murmuring swells,
        My heart is tuned to prayer.

    In Sunday garb, all neatly clad,
        With joy upon each face,
    The dame and sire, and lass and lad,
        Approach the holy place.

    'Tis true, in yonder sacred fane
        I cannot praise my King;
    Yet in the meadow and the lane
        I will be worshiping.

And, while I pray, a sweet response
        Shall rise from every stream,
    And all the little birds at once
        Shall chant the morning hymn.

Oh, what a charm reigns o'er the scene,
        Beneath those dappled skies!
    The cattle wear a pious mien,
        And earth is paradise.

I ask no priests 'neath fretted dome
Their holy prayers to read,
No pew beside the marble tomb,
When God is over-head.

So here, beneath His loving eye,
I'll worship and adore;
The vaulted heaven my canopy,
The earth my temple floor.

from THE POET'S GRAVE

Near a village church, and shady grove,
Where I've listened to Janie's tale of love;
Where the mournful yew, with its branches spread,
Shadows the mansions of the dead;
Where the death-toned bell, with its vibrous toll,
May strike on the prayerless, hopeless soul,
Till he thinks as he never thought before;
Till he feels that his pride is light and poor;
Poor when compared with the shortest breath,
And light in the balances of death:
Where the swain may leave his humble cot,
To visit one who shall be not;
And nymphs at eventide may stray,
Their tearful homage oft to pay,
And dress my grave with simple flowers,
To be refreshed by heavenly showers —

Near there!

On the lonely brow of yonder hill,
Where the bright and tiny singing rill
Leaps o'er its washed and pebbled bed,
As it comes from its moss-lipped fountain-head,
Speeding into the river below,

Where the clouds are reflected, white as snow;
Where the boatman, as he glides along,
May look upward and chant his plaintive song,
Singing my dirge; with the waving tree
As Nature's sweetest symphony —

Just there!

Yes, when the pale moon sheds her light
O'er the grassy turf at the birth of night,
They shall wander near and gently tread
On the tufted knoll of my narrow bed,
And, sighing, say as they pensive look,
"The fields were his study and nature his book;
He loved to pen in simple rhyme
His thoughts of the beautiful and sublime,
And learnt to admire as well as read
The works of the great and mighty dead;
Whilst at the fireside he'd rehearse
The thoughts which he had writ in verse,
Some sentiments would grace his song,
And please as with an Angel's tongue;
Some touched the tenderest sympathy,
And caused a painful harmony."
Then ne'er despise his humble strain,
Who writes to please ne'er wrote in vain.
Affection's tribute they shall pay,

Let fall a tear and go their way,
Saying, "he would have shed his blood
For his country's weal, as the cause of God."
Farewell! I make my last request,
When death shall chill my Janie's breast,
Like two doves let us sleep in one hallowed nest,
And the question ask no more, then, where?
'Neath the hawthorn tree, we'll be buried there!
Yes, there—Yes, there!

THE LION-FLAG OF ENGLAND

The lion-flag of England!
Say, Britons, shall it wave,
The scorn of every base-born serf,
And jest of every slave;
A sign to tell them how they beat
The bravest of the earth,
And teach them by our England's fate
To magnify their worth?
"Forbid it, Heav'n," the nations cry,
In council gravely met;
"We'll send her aid across the seas,
And she shall conquer yet."

Have faith in dear Old England!
A voice comes from her slain;
"We found her sound enough at heart,
But erring in the brain."
Have patience, and Old Time shall prove
Her power is like her oak,
Which rises in the scale of worth
Beneath the deadly stroke.
For, though she staggers at the blow
Her hero-bands have met—

Her ancient prowess gives the pledge
That she shall conquer yet.

Have faith in dear Old England!
Her lion-hearts lie dead;
But tens of thousands ready wait
To battle in their stead.
They know from history's reddest page,
That nations, when opprest,
Must point their swords for arguments
Against the tyrant's breast.
While voices from the grand old past
Come pleading—"Pay your debt:
For you we fought—defend our fame,
And you shall conquer yet."

Who would not fight for England,
A-field or on the main,
And try to win (if she has lost)
Her honour back again?
The creature who would dare refuse
To take his country's part,
Is coward—slave—an ingrate vile,
A traitor at the heart!
And little thinks what he enjoys
Was bought with blood and sweat,

Or such who sheath their swords to rust
May see Siberia yet.

O England! dear Old England!
What land is like to thee,—
So rich in patriotic gems,
And free as thou art free?
Who quenched the bigot's faggot-fire?
Who stanched the patriot's blood?
Who? England, at the battle-cry
Of "Liberty and God!"
Her Past! why 'tis a deathless fame,
A sun that cannot set;—
A power majestic—and her name
Shall serve to conquer yet!

"God bless our dear Old England,"
I heard my father pray:
"The brightest gem in Christendom,"
I heard my mother say.
And then they took me on their knee,
And pressed my little hand,
And told me of the Northmen's fate,
And Alfred's sturdy band;
And how on Northam's sea-girt plain
The Dane and Saxon met,

And prophesied that bloody times
Would come for England yet.

In daisy-quilted England
I've made the twain a bed!
And 'mong the words I've treasured up,
The sweetest which they said
Were, "England, dear Old England!
Who dare her honour mar?"
She'd rather bind a broken heart
Than break a heart in war.
They said she never fought for sport,
Nor burned to prove her might;—
Was much in love with harvest swords,
And only fought for Right;
And how this island in the sea
Is like a beacon set,
To light the world to liberty,
And make her glorious yet.

"Hurrah! for dear Old England!"
Our gallant fellows cry;
They shout it in the deadly breach,
And where they wounded lie.
They wear the charm about their necks,
As maidens wear their curls;

They treasure up its memories
As princes treasure pearls;
And while they breathe the last fond thoughts
For those they can't forget,
The accents die upon their lips—
"Ay—we—shall—conquer yet!"

Hurrah! for dear Old England!
Come, Britons, one and all,
Strike on, strike hard, strike home, strike sure,
Till WAR himself shall fall;
Till Time, on pointing finger wears
The precious pearl of Peace,
And Earth sends up her anthem-shout
That loving hearts increase:
Fight on, keep heart, look up, be firm;
And never once forget
That Heaven proclaims this God-stamped truth,
"The Right shall conquer yet."

'TIS PRIMROSE TIME AGAIN

*T*he sun is smiling on the day;
And, high upon the wing,
The lark pours forth his sweetest lay
Into the ear of Spring.
The lusty thrush, in merry mood,
Pipes out his loudest strain;
And children shout, from wood to wood,
"'Tis primrose time again."

The willow buds are swathed in down;
The hazel is in bloom ;
The hawthorn wears a richer brown;
And greener grows the broom.
Hark, every bird, in bush and tree,
Cries, "Must we sing in vain?
Come out, ye brick-bound souls, be free—
'Tis primrose time again."

"Come, wife, my love, away—away
To mossy cave and bower;
Or let us in our shadows play
With Nature one short hour.
Thou and the wee folk now are well,

To-morrow it may rain;
My heart is ringing like a bell,
"'Tis primrose time again."

THE OLD STONE-BREAKER

Christ befriend thee, poor old man,
With misty eye, and fleshless bone,
Dripping and shivering there alone,
Wrapped in a rag on that cold, cold stone;
Feeble and toothless, haggard and wan,
My heart aches for thee, poor old man.

A stranded wreck by life's rough sea,
The old man raised his eyes and said,
"'Tis a sin to wish that one were dead;
But days together I want for bread;
And Sir, oh Sir, the wretch you see,
Ne'er dreamt he should so aged be."

"Yonder's the parish house," said I,
"And one so poor and very old
Should seek its refuge from the cold."
"No jail for me, were it built of gold, —
I ever loved the fields and sky;
I would rather sit by this hedge and die.

"When I was young, my sturdy prime
I sold for very nought a week —

A shilling-a-day—the truth I speak,
And my wife and little ones oft were sick;
And now, with my head all white with rime,
You see a victim of ill-paid time.

"'Tis hard to starve; I sought 'the board';
They chided me much for being poor;
My memory called up days of yore,
When I made the wood ring and threshing-floor;
And I thought of many a golden hoard,
These shrivelled hands for them had stored.

"My spirit was broken; I turned to go,
When a rough voice thundered, 'Pauper, stay!'
And spoke of an order for three-pence a day:
I have sixpence each week for lodgings to pay;
That is two-pence per day for the six, Sir, you know,
And the seventh I feast on the thoughts of my woe."

"What is thy pittance, poor old man?
The price of those blows on that stubborn stone,
That crack, crack, crack, and constant groan?"
" Two-pence a day," quoth he, with a moan.
Down o'er my cheeks the big tear ran,
And I pitied the fate of that poor old man.

Ye who are wealthy, a lesson learn,—
Hear what the blessed Jesus said,
"Give us each day our daily bread";
And drive out want from the poor man's shed:
Work him, but love him, and pay him in turn,
And the aged for hunger shall cease to mourn.

Would you have England without a brand?
Would you have Devon the merry shire?
See that each poor old withered sire,
Doomed on its bosom soon to expire,
Dies not an outcast, hammer in hand,
While there's corn in your garner, and gold in the land.

AN AUTUMN INVITATION

Come out into the woodlands, love,
Before the trees are bare;
The woodlark singeth on the hill
His sweetly mellow air.

A smile is seen on Autumn's cheek,
As one who hath a store;
The bees are in the ivy-bloom,
Above the abbey door.

Come out, before the dark days come,
With blasts and heavy rains:
Come out, before the winter binds
The earth in icy chains.

The air is soft as eider-down;
And brown October's eye
Is looking out to woo thee forth
Beneath its sapphire sky.

A few sweet flow'rets linger still,
Which Summer left behind;
And still a lingering violet
Is swaying in the wind.

Once more, I pray thee, love, come out,
Where happy woodlarks sing,
And dream, while listening to their notes,
You hear the birds of Spring.

THE LITTLE SCARE-CROW

She is up in yonder field,

Mid the new-sown corn;
She'll be there until the eve,
She has been there since the morn.
O, the pretty little creature,
With her bright blue eye,
I heard her noisy clapper,
And her scare-crow cry.

I paused to mark the child -
She was very pale and young;
She told me "she was six,"
With her merry little tongue.
In her hand she held her hat,
Which the wild wind swayed;
And purple were the feet
Of the scare-crow maid.

More happy than a queen,
Though scanty was her food,
The child that sang her song
To that clapper-music rude.
This the maiden's simple lay,

As she warbled in her nook,
"Here, clapping every day,
I scare the robber-rook!"

from "WOODLANDS"

I know a cottage perched upon a hill;
A sylvan home, a nest among the trees,
Where oft the clatter of a neighbouring mill
Goes murmuring up upon the friendly breeze;
In sooth, so rural is that lovely cot,
The wind, the mill, and ringing anvil's clink,
And fisher's song beside the river's brink,
And ploughboy's whistle, and the lime-team's trot,
And milkmaid's carol o'er her luscious drink,
Are the chief sounds that reach that blissful spot:

Save when the linnets' chorus streameth down,
And bleating flocks and cattle wake the lea,
When thrushes warble in the elm tree's crown,
And skylarks, through dense showers of harmony,
Mount up, and soar above the happy throngs,
To sport awhile among the cloudlets white; -
What joy! to hear them in their circling flight,
Trilling their love-notes with their merry tongues,
Paving their pathways with their own sweet songs;
Birds spurning earth, air-birds, and winged with light.

It sits so high, that ere the Yeo, a stream
That stealeth by it, creeping to the sea,
Is lighted with the virgin morning's beam,
Its windows sparkle bright and silverly;
Not only does it win the earliest kiss
Of sunny morning's sweet and rosy mouth,
But all the balmy odours of the south
Conspire to make it one dear scene of bliss;
No accent there is heard of speech uncouth,
Nor do its inmates one pure pleasure miss.

There is a pathway winding up the steep,
O'erhung with chestnut-bloom and sycamore,
The woodbines there in forms fantastic creep,
And primrose tufts and mosses strew the floor;
The thorn blows there, and holly overgrown
With ivy, bearing many-shapen leaves,
Which some sweet wood-nymph in the noontide weaves,
Or when the Night her mantle dark has thrown
Over the gold and purple of the eves,
Or at the twilight of the infant dawn.

The clematis, the sorrel, and wild brier,
Wood-briony, and brambles, flourish there;
There summer zephyrs fan the poppy's fire,
And heath, and gorse, and dog-rose scent the air.

A shelter from the cold North's biting wind,
The partridge seeks its broad and sunny glade,
The pheasant lodges in its ample shade;
And pies, the robbers of the feathery kind,
Th' aerial homes of squirrels oft invade,
And there the bees their sweetest blossoms find.

O blest retreat, green haunt of poesy,
There I could dwell a studious solitaire,
And, nestled in thy bower of melody,
Forego the pleasures which the world deems rare.
I only ask to see the spreading dale
That sleeps below thy bristling, pine-girt base,
To hear the horn and view the lively chase,
And watch the sea-gull ride upon the gale;
Or mark the leaping of the silver dace
In Tor's bright waters dancing down the vale.

THE RIVER

From its sedge-lipped fountain flowing,
Down the hill-side, through the vale,
By the cottage, meadow, orchard,
Telling one delightful tale.
Dimpling, whirling, dancing, purling,
Sweetly babbling in its course;
Bright and happy, wandering minstrel,
Singing of its native source.
God the fount, and Love the river,
Even so our life should be,
Ever blessing, praising ever,
One perpetual melody.

A MAYTIME WISH

I would the world could see thee as I behold thee, May,
  With eyes like sapphires gleaming through the
  orchards by the way,
   With the campion and the crowfoot on thy
   daisy-jewell'd vest,
  And a wreath of apple blossoms dropping down
   upon thy breast.

  I would all eyes could see thee as I behold thee now,
   With the woodruff and the bluebell, and the lily on
     thy brow;
   With thy kirtle richly purfled with the gorse's golden
     boss,
And the orchis and the violet, the primrose and the moss.

  I would all ears could listen to thy merry-making, May,
   Could listen as I listen to thy happy roundelay;
  Then a louder song would greet us from thy orchestra of
     leaves,
  For fewer birds would break their hearts because of little
     thieves.

A form of life and beauty, I see thee, lovely May,
Breathing balm upon the meadows from each sweetly
scented spray;
From the lilac and the hawthorn, and the furze upon the
down,
And the wall-flower by the wayside in its dress of
cottage-brown.

Would you see her as I see her, you must be where
I have been,
Where the oak-tree, and the elm-tree, and the
beechen tree are seen;
Where the bright and silvery poplars in their leafy
beauty shine,
And the bees are quaffing deeply from their chalices
of wine.

You must linger, as I linger, in the shadow of each nook,
You must listen, as I listen, to the prattle of the brook;
You must woo her, as I woo her, with a bosom full
of love,
And the maid will stand before you like a vision
from above.

THE BRACKEN IS SPRINGING
SONG

The bracken is springing, my Janie, I see,
And curling its droplets all golden for thee;
The oak's budding branches with leaflets are brown,
And Nature is out in her green cottage gown.

There's balm in the air, love, and bloom on the trees,
And warbling of woodlands, and humming of bees;
While bright are the meadows and sunny the skies,
And everywhere glory to gladden the eyes.

Yet, Janie my darling, there's something beside
The fields in their beauty, the woods in their pride,
To give me the pleasure my soul would desire,
Thy presence, dear Janie, my song to inspire.

Oh, cruel it is to imprison those charms,
That rose on thy cheek, and that bud in thy arms;
Come out in the sunlight, here roses should blow,
And give me the Eden I covet below.

A COT AT WEARGIFFORD AND JANIE FOR ME

SONG

Sigh not for honour, I covet not station,
A man may be noble, though lowly his birth,
The world's my domain, and my home is creation,
And proud as a monarch I traverse the earth.
Yet still there's a wish in my bosom I cherish,
I long for a spot where the soul may be free;
A fig for ambition, and gold let it perish,
A cot at Weargifford and Janie for me.

Sweet vale of green Devon, wood-shelter'd and cosy,
How blest are thy maidens, and happy thy men!
Thy little ones all, like thy gardens, are rosy,
Thy orchards are fruitful, and fertile thy plain!
Long, long may thy hall throw its shade on the river,
The beautiful Tor winding up from the sea—
Thy woods, herds, and flocks, and thy sunsets for ever,
A cot at Weargifford and Janie for me.

And O, the sweet bees and their hives full of honey!
And O, the gay warblers that pipe there in spring!
And O, the fair banks and their blossoms so bonny!
And the sweet village bells with their ding-a-dong-ding!

I hate to be bound by the fetters of fashion,
The town hath its chains for the soul that is free,
My love for dear Nature was ever a passion,
A cot at Weargifford and Janie for me.

THE "HOBBY," CLOVELLY

They told me 'twas enchanted ground,
    The fairies' sweetest ferny haunt;
    I deem'd it but an empty sound,
        A fancy, or an idle vaunt.

But when I pass'd its rustic gate,
My Muse, all buoyant, spread her wing,
    And Melody, with joy elate,
        In ecstasy began to sing —

Of beautiful and balmy spots,
    And pathways buried in the shade;
    Of sultry nooks and cooling grots,
And flowers that gem the sunny glade;

Of trees depending, till the leaves
Rest on the roadway's rocky ground,
Where hares disport at summer eves,
    Ere they into the dingles bound;

Bright glimpses of the Severn sea,
    Like its reflected heaven at rest,
    Where Lundy in serenity
    Sleeps like an island of the blest;

Of broad sea-plains of meadowy green,
And witching peeps of cove and pier,
And boats that dot the liquid scene
Of blue and purpling waters near;

Of rich oak-bosses on each height,
And rills that ripple down the glen,
Now foaming into purest white,
Now running into gloom agen;

Of deep ravines and hollow coombs,
Of foxglove banks and ferny dells,
And a fair bay which ever booms
Its music as the ocean swells;

And hawks that wildly screaming, wheel
Around each rude and savage cliff,
And sea-birds, that with downy keel
Skim o'er the billows like a skiff;

And trawlers which, like butterflies,
Flit o'er the main with tawny wing,
And barks whose topmasts pierce the skies,
And breakers ever murmuring;

And a bluff rock with thorny crown,
A shelter for the timid fawn,
And woods for ever sloping down,
As smooth to sight as shaven lawn;

A village like a waterfall,
Or torrent rushing to the tide,
Where brawny fishers, stout and tall,
Trip laughing down its craggy side;

Quaint bridges hung with mossy curls,
Where strings of polish'd ivy shine,
And troops of merry dark-eyed girls,
Who boast a beauty half divine.

My numbers fail — no human eye
A sweeter spot shall e'er behold;
And truth must utter with a sigh,
Not half its glory can be told!

The sylvan pomp and majesty,
Which there in harmony have met;
The bay which, in the neighbouring sea,
A sapphire seems in em'rald set,

Enslave the vision and the thought,
As charm on charm is quick reveal'd,
Till pleasure is to rapture wrought,
And language is in silence seal'd.

THE TORRIDGE

I have seen thee in thy glory, like a virgin in her pride,
 When a myriad suns were flashing on the bosom of
   thy tide,
As the arm of the Atlantic, stretching inward from the bay,
 Roll'd its wave along the golden sands that pave
  thy water-way.

 I have seen thee when the May-time, in her frock of
   Whitsun-white,
  Strew'd thy banks with red rimm'd daisy flowers,
  like broken clouds of light;
And in Summer, when the cattle cool'd their hot hides in
   the stream,
  And thy white town on the hillside look'd the picture
  of a dream.

 In Autumn, too, I've watch'd thee, when the ragged
   woods that slope
  Beneath thy undulating heights seem'd like a
  wither'd hope;
And in Winter, when the heavy clouds were tempest-
   rent and grey,
  And thy torrent, like a troubled soul, roll'd on its
  turbid way.

In the morn, when the town lattices were rich with
golden fire —
At the noontide, when thy wavelets brush'd the old
bridge like a lyre —
In the even, when the dreamy sun behind the hill
went down—
And at night-time, when old Bideford made thee a
brilliant crown.

I have loved thee when thy shipping threw its shadows
o'er thy face,
As the stars came out all silently along the realms of space;
But when the moon was mirror'd on thy ripples
softly bright,
With a passion I have worshipp'd thee, my beauty
and delight.

And had I but an artist's hand, I'd paint some
pleasant scene
Of thy iris-tinted waters in their richest summer sheen,
When our little ones like love gods are sporting in
thine arms,
And I'd envy not the lover of the Yarrow and its charms.

A NOVEMBER SCENE

It was a soft November eve and a faint yellow dye,
Pale as a winter primrose, ting'd the margin of the sky,
While leaves, like brown-wing'd butterflies, came eddying
     from the oak,
          And spiral shafts of purest blue curl'd up of
          cottage smoke.

     Would half that evening's splendour in language
          could be told;—
     The clouds that gather'd in the west were all ablaze
          with gold,
     Then rich reflected crimson lights, like those we see
          in dew,
          Fell on the ruby-tinted beech, that stood beneath
          my view.

Away to seaward, lofty crags of snowy cloud were seen,
     Whose amber tops glow'd like a fire against the
          blue serene;
     And inland, where the umber slopes lay underneath
          the east,
     The sunset flash'd its glory on the ploughman and
          his beast.

No murmur of the forest mock'd the murmur of the sea,
Nor wanton wind went whispering, or wooing in the tree,
    The only note that met the ear was the sweet
    cheery sound,
  Which a young maiden made to call the swine in
    from the ground;—

    Save, where the feet went rustling among the
    crumpled leaves,
   Or when a sparrow chirp'd above the stack's
   o'er-hanging eaves,
   Or where the starlings cut the air as, in their
   homeward flight,
They sought the reedy plashets, there to nestle for a night.

 Now peering o'er a patch of cloud, as curly as a fleece,
The moon is seen surveying all below in rest and peace,
    Until her face grows golden, as the neighbouring
    elm-tree's crown,
Then softens to a silvery tone when the red sun is down.

    Such beauty heaven and earth supplies, for those
    who wander out
To see what Providence has done, and Nature is about;
And dull must be that mortal man who, traversing our sod,
Sees not the wonder-working hand of an Almighty God.

UNDER THE SNOW

Sweet little loving thing, low, low, low,
Down in the cold, cold grave she lies;
Deep 'neath the daisy-knoll under the snow,
Silenced for ever her carols and cries.

Sweet little Dimpled-chin, how she would dance!
Dear little Laughing-eyes, how she would smile!
Still are her tiny feet now, and her glance
Beams not on me for a weary long while.

"Dead!" do my neighbours say? Death is a dream:
In the mid-Maytime she went out to play;
Daily I see her by meadow and stream,
Couch'd 'mid the goldencups, sunny as they.

Weep, my eyes, scalding tears, weep, weep, weep!
Bleed, my soul; throb, my heart, heavy with pain!
When shall my tender one wake from her sleep?
When shall I gaze on my beauty again?

Sweet little loving thing, low, low, low,
Down in the cold, cold grave she lies;
Deep 'neath the daisy-knoll under the snow,
Silenced for ever her carols and cries.

THE VISION

You wonder, stranger, why I smiled,
And think I am distraught;
Just then the vision of my child
My tender fancy caught.

That little corner pane you see
Up in that window there,
Is far more precious unto me
Than gems, however rare!

Thither each morn my darling came
And smiled her bright good-bye!
The sweetest picture in a frame
That ever met my eye.

Methinks I hear her tapping now
To give me one kiss more,
Her lips all laughter, and her brow
With gladness running o'er.

So oft beside my garden gate,
Ere starting on my way,
I turn, my soul with joy elate,
To see her at her play.

Thus memory will ever strive
To cheat old ruthless Death,
While Love my lost one keeps alive
With his immortal breath.

Marine Gardens, Bideford

THE ANNIVERSARY

Twelve weary moons have run their round,
Since in her winding-sheet we bound
And laid our lily underground—
Our lily o' the May,
And yet we gather here in tears,
With throbbing hearts and listening ears;
And as we bend above the dead,
We conjure up another bed
Where our sweet infant lay.

Yes, we do prize our poor dead dove,
And though the stars die out above,
There's nought shall quench our flame of love,
Or dull its sacred light.
And long as blossoms grace the spring,
And golden-pinioned finches sing,
For her sweet sake we'll come and strew
Upon her grave her violets blue,
And daisies silver-white.

With arrowy dartings here and there,
The screaming swifts shoot through the air,
So did they when Death sought our fair,

And blanched her comely bloom.
True heralds they of pale decay,
Though only in the sun they play;
For when the May-bush is most sweet,
And lilacs scent the city street,
Our fairest fill the tomb.

TO BIDEFORD,
IN PROSPECT OF LEAVING IT

And must I leave thee, my adopted home,
Nurse of my inspiration and my vaunt,
Thy broad strands silver'd with the salt sea-foam,
Each fairy inlet and each sylvan haunt?

What visions of blue skies, and purple hills,
And ocean-plains will rise upon my view!
And O, what melodies of birds and rills
Will fill the silence when I sigh, Adieu!

I cannot say farewell without a tear;
My spirit bleeds to think that we must part:
Yet there are claims more sacred and more dear
Than thine enchantments, darling of my heart!

Oft in my dreams, when far away from thee,
Amid thy matchless charms my soul shall stray,
To list the music of some wandering bee,
Or mark the sea-gull sporting in the bay.

Watching the stars burn through the silent sky,
Or the moon trembling in the rippled flood;
Or listening to the tempest's lullaby
To drowsy Nature in a neighbouring wood.

Treading again the valley of the Yeo,
A dreamer in the deepening hush of eve;
Or gliding where the waters gently flow
Beneath the shadow of sweet Oldiscleave.

Perchance the pilgrim by me hither led
Shall thread thy paths and syllable my name,
And talk of days when on thy banks I led
My dark-eyed joys, and married thee to fame.

'Twas here I felt that sweet, oppressive power,
Which beauty treasures up in solitude,
The Godhead's presence in the simplest flower,
The poet's passion and his gratitude.

Weak was my praise, but what I had I gave,
As some return for my continuous joy;
And when the minstrel slumbers in his grave,
Think of him kindly for his loved employ.

For each dumb beauty I have found a voice,
Thy peasants bless me in their uncouth tongue,
Thy merry maidens in my lays rejoice,
And all thy rivers warble in my song.

Yes, I do love thee, and if I forget
How much I owe thee, let my right hand fail

To prove its cunning, till the countless debt
Is wiped away by some melodious tale.

TAMMIE'S TOKEN.

 Rose from Lincombe by the sea!
To say that Tammie thinks o' me.
The gales that wanton in the South
Still linger in its dainty mouth,
So odorous, that all the room
Is fragrant with its rich perfume.
Go, get you down to Lover's Dell
For water from the dripping well,
While as some small return that she
Has favoured me all bards above,
I give it in a melody,
The immortality of love,—
As Moore and Milton would have done,
Had they beheld so fair a one.

MY LATEST PUBLICATION

My dear brother BURRITT, you asked me to-day,
If the muse was propitious and jingling away.
Well, yes; she is lively; how can she be less?
To tell you the truth, friend, I'm just out of press.
My work has been published by Mattock and Hoe,
And brought out in hawthorn, embossed with the sloe;
And, if I am spared in a healthy condition,
Next summer shall see out another edition.

"Well, what is the title?" I hear you inquire;
"An Essay on Nature," which you will admire.
When first I commenced, it was tug, tug and toil;
A spade was my steel pen, my paper the soil.
But after a scratch or two made with good will,
I found that my metal would write like a quill.
As thoughts from a thought, friend, will oftentimes breed,
So charlock in acres is raised from one seed.

"Ill weeds grow apace;" and, to kill out the crop,
I burnt it together with "scutch" on the top.
Next into the ground with a purpose I went,
Till over my task all aweary I bent;
And found that my thoughts sought expression in lines

All dotted with quaint hieroglyphical signs.
'Tis true, I first purposed commencing in prose,
When, finding a cabbage was but a green rose,
I started in verse, and discovered that greens
Was a very fair rhyme after carrots for beans;
And talk about fancy, why look at my peas;
I've old "Dan, the Irishman," blowing at ease:
While "Progress" is seen in "Mc Clean's" great
"Advancer,"
As well as his "Wonderful," such a sweet dancer!
For "Champions" of all sorts I have an affection,
And therefore I glory in "Veitch's Perfection."
I have stanzas of lettuce, and parsnips, and leeks,
And a canto of onions, a study for weeks.
I have sonnets of celery, turnips and sage:
And sweet mint and savory—what a sweet page!
I have raspberries blushing like love on their stalks,
And strawberries creeping all over the walks;
And, if you are loyal, 'twill gladden your sight
To see my potatoes—red, purple, and white:
There are "Regents," "Victorias," "Prince Rocks,"
and "King Flooks,"
And a host of "self-setters" abloom in the nooks.
The bright "scarlet runner"—a fancy run wild—
Is having her fling like a frolicsome child;
While the artichoke lifts up her head to the sky,

As if in proud scorn of the marrows hard by;
And as for my parsley, 'twill just suit your mood,
'Tis such a sweet miniature, friend, of a wood.
So much for the matter my new book contains,
A work of the muscles far more than the brains;
And maybe 'twill please you to learn by the way,
That the critics have not had an ill word to say.
Thanks, thanks to a rake that revised all for me,
Not the sign of an unfinished thought can you see;
"A work," the reviewers say, "suiting the taste."
Yours aye in good fellowship,—E. C.

In haste.

Rock Cottage,
Moorpool Lane, Harborne, 1866

IT'S O! TO BE IN DEVON AT THE MERRY CHRISTMAS-TIME

Now the days are dark and dreary,

And the year is growing weary,

And the leaves have left the branches

Of the sycamore and lime;

I am thinking of thy bounty,

My dear old native county.

It's O! to be in Devon at the Merry Christmas-time.

Who that has seen thy daughters,

And the flashing of thy waters,

And hears thy name the music

Of some olden English rhyme;

And pines not for thy alleys

And river-lighted valleys?

It's O! to be in Devon at the Merry Christmas-time.

Here the bough that we are lopping,

Here the snowflake in its dropping,

Here the flocks that roam the pastures,

Are blackened with the grime;

And the cottages, and hedges,

And the grasses, and the sedges.

It's O! to be in Devon at the Merry Christmas-time.

There each cosy hearth is glowing,

And the honey-wine is flowing;

While the frost-work on the lattice

Is melting like the rime;

And the lads the moors are pacing,

The hare and rabbit tracing.

It's O! to be in Devon at the Merry Christmas-time.

And village waits are singing,

And village bells are ringing;

From hill to hill they answer

With the old familiar chime:

And the holly's reddest coral.

Is smiling by the laurel.

It's O! to be in Devon at the Merry Christmas-time.

I hear each good man boasting
Of the "round" his dame is roasting,
From the ox or maiden-heifer,
That was slaughtered in its prime;
And I see the fat geese spinning,
And the ancient games beginning.
It's O! to be in Devon at the Merry Christmas-time.

There's the crumpet, and the pippin,
And the brown ale for the "flip" in,
And the hot toast for the cider:—
Would that envy were no crime;
And the ashen faggot hissing,
And the mistletoe for kissing.
It's O! to be in Devon at the Merry Christmas-time.

O! sweet haunt of the pheasant,
My home-land fair and pleasant;
Though the music of the nightingale
Be foreign to thy clime,
More charming is thy greeting

Of the guests at festal meeting.

God bless thee, dear old Devon, with a Merry
Christmas-time!

Harborne, Christmas, 1869

GREAT THOUGHTS

reat thoughts, like high tides, lift us up from the slime
And sludge of the world, with its garbage and grime;
And bear us away, where the soul is as free
And pure as the Guillemot riding the sea.

AUGUST

There's a mist o'er the meadow-land, mountain
and stream,
Young Morning has not yet awoke from her dream;
Mute Poesy muses in peace by the mill,
And the trees are but shadowy clouds on the hill.

How rich the delight! there's a charm in the time,
The honey's aroma is sweet in the lime;
And a fairy like music, most welcome to me,
For a harper's abroad in the merry brown bee.

What a hush! for a season, e'en labour is still,
And nothing is heard but the tink of a rill,
Or the sparrow's sharp chirp, as it strikes on the ear,
And the clarion challenge of bold chanticleer.

Alone I am monarch and lord of the sky!
The bird is my piper; my hall is on high;
And the landscape, that stretches away to the blue,
Is mine, by my birthright, with rapture to view.

In Barlow's Road, Harborne, 1878

A SIGH FOR DEVON

Bright haunt of the daffodil, myrtle, and rose,
Of solitude sweet, and of pleasant repose,
Where a welcome waits all with a heart in its hand,
My Devon! dear Devon! my beautiful land!
May death ne'er for thee draw a shaft from his quiver,
I loved thee, do love, and shall love thee for ever.

Dear home of my fathers, when thinking of thee,
In fancy I often am down by the sea,
On old Northam Burrows, or Woolacombe sands,
Where Robert the phantom is twisting his bands.
Then deem me no runaway-ingrate, O never!
First love of my heart, I shall love thee for ever.

When summer is come, and the welkin is fair,
There's something of paradise everywhere;
But bloom in perfection, and nature in tune,
Are thine, O Devonia! in beautiful June.
Blest region of valley, hill, woodland, and river,
I love thee, dear land, and shall love thee for ever.

The meadows o' Warwick are dainty and sweet,
And the fair fields o' Staffordshire, soft to the feet;

But for rich mossy sward, sunny upland, and glen,
Lane, coppice, and stream, give me Devon again.
Yes! soul-bound to thee, which no fate can dissever,
I love thee, dear land, and shall love thee for ever.

Thanks Memory, nurse o' my fancy and hope,
I feel I am now where the combes are aslope,
While innocent lovers are telling their tale,
At Barricane beach and in Collipriest vale,
Where my Exe from the moorland weds Lowman's
fair river:—
Sweet land of my love! I shall love thee for ever.

THE MESSAGE FROM THE SEA

All night, the wild tumultuous main
With loud and angry roar,
Had strove to dash the bark, in vain,
On Baggy's deadly shore;
But at the breaking of the day,
She rode triumphant in the bay.

As midships the bold skipper stood,
And the mad breakers eyed,
Which leapt like furies o'er the flood,
He slapp'd the good ship's side,
And swore, by all he held most dear,
With her he nothing had to fear.

He was the foremost in the prow
Upon her gala day,
When the fair figure on her bow
First kiss'd the briny spray,
And his brave heart with pride beat high,
As like a bird he felt her fly.

"Hurrah! hurrah! she rides it well;"
The sturdy landsmen sing,

While plunging in the seething swell
They mark her labouring;
And as by Morte she ploughs her way,
"Heaven send her safe," the watchers pray.

Another night, a starless sky,
A levin-lighted sea,
And near the dawn a crash and cry,
The good ship, where is she?
The waif-strewn beach is white with foam,
Where anxious waiters early roam.

When glistening in the bladder-wrack,
Just thrown on Northam's strand,
They saw, with many a star and crack,
A bottle on the sand, —
Which a young fisher-lad, for play,
Kick'd thoughtlessly along his way.

"Hold hard my boy," an old man cried,
A weather-beaten tar.
As he a tiny scroll espied
Beside a stranded spar,
While a young maiden, flushed with fear,
Stood half in dread the news to hear.

Then turning to the girl said he
" 'For Polly, with my love,'
It is a message from the sea,
Which sad to thee will prove,
And thus it reads, 'Just going down,
Brig, Betsy, Captain, Caleb Brown,' "

When she beside the seething bay,
Dropt dead upon the shore;
And now a phantom haunts for aye
The sands of Appledore,
Which mariners oft see in white.
And sigh "Poor Polly walks to night."

LAYS FOR THE LITTLE ONES

THE DUCKLING

Old Mother Cubidee went for a walk,
With her seven little chickens and one little duck,
Amusing them all with her old-fashioned talk,
Clickity, clackity, clock, cluck, cluck, —

Till she came to a pool by the side of a road,
With her seven little chickens and one little duck,
When ducky plunged in where the water was broad,
Clickity, clackity, clockity, cluck.

The hen she looked on with her little ones near,
The seven little chickens amazed at the duck,
Till she felt every feather a-quiver with fear,
Clickity, clackity, clockity, cluck.

The little rogue floated around and around,
Then stood on his head, did the wee little duck,
While the hen screamed aloud with despair in the sound,
Clickity, clackity, clockity, cluck.

And now standing up on the water so deep,
And flapping his winglets, the dear little duck,

He gave a loud laugh, then he took a wild leap;
Clickity, clackity, clockity, cluck.

His sport being over he paddled to land,
As if it were nothing, the quaint little duck;
When the hen gave a chuckle of joy to her band,
Clickity, clackity, clock, cluck, cluck.

THE SONG OF THE PEWIT

I'm little Petawin Pewit,
And live out on the moor,
In a pretty little grass house,
With peat-turf for my door.
I can't sing like the thrushes,
I often wish I could,
Nor warble like the linnets
That live within the wood;
But then I do the best I can,
As mine have done before,
And gaily wave my graceful wing
When speeding o'er the moor,
Singing ever as I fly,

"Life is very sweet,
Pewit witity, pewit witity,
Pewit, witityweet."

When comes the time for buttercups,
And bluebells, in my nest
I sit amid the sedgy tufts
And plume my shining breast;
Or saying "Good-bye, darling,"
Unto my little wife,
I pass the woods and meadows
And lead a pleasant life —
In finding for our baby-birds
The simple food they need
Then hasten to my home again
Rejoicing in my deed,
Singing ever as I fly,
"Life is very sweet,
Pewit witity, pewit witity.
Pewit, witityweet."

DEVONSHIRE CREAM

Sweeter than the odours borne on southern gales,
Comes the clotted nectar of my native vales,
Bright and golden crusted, rich beyond compare -
Food on which a goddess evermore may fare.
Burns may praise his haggis, Horace sing of wine,
Hunt of Hybla-honey, which he deem'd divine,
But in the Elysiums of the poet's dream
Where is the delicious without Devon-cream?

Talk of peach or melon, quince or jargonel,
White-water, black hamburg, or the muscatel,
Pippin or pomegranate, apricot or pine,
Greengages or strawberries, or our elder-wine;
Take them all and welcome, yes the whole, say I,
Ay! And even junket, mince and mazzard pie,
Only let our lasses, like the morning, gleam
Joyous with their skimmers full of clouted cream.

What a host of pictures crowd upon my sight
As I view the luscious feast of my delight!
Meadows fram'd in hawthorn, coppices in green,
Village fanes on hill-tops, crowning every scene,
Buttercups, and cattle clad in coats of red,

Flocks in daisy pastures, couples newly wed,
Happy in their homesteads, by a flashing stream;
But what is this golden, crimp'd and mellow cream? –

Quintessence of sunshine, gorse and broomy-lea,
Privet and carnation, violet and pea,
Meadow-sweet and primrose, honeysuckle, briar,
Lily, mint and jasmine, stock and gilly-spire,
Woodruff, rose and clover, sycamore and lime,
Myrtle and magnolia, daffodil and thyme,
Is our pearl of dainties – and, to end my theme;
Nature's choice confection is Devonia's cream.

THE POSTMAN POET

Liz Shakespeare

As a young boy, Edward Capern is desperate to read and write, but has to work an eighty-hour week in Barnstaple's lace factory. As a man, he dreams of writing poetry and building a fairer society, but these aspirations cannot put food on the table. He fears he will never be able to marry Jane, the woman he loves, and it is her skill as a milliner that eventually provides enough for them to set up a simple home together in Bideford.

Edward's fortunes change when he finds employment as a postman. As he walks the Devon lanes, he begins to write poems and songs that express his delight in the countryside and the people he meets, but neither he nor Jane can foresee the profound impact his poetry will have on their lives.

Liz Shakespeare's novel draws on historical research and Capern's own writing to tell the story of Bideford's Postman Poet from obscurity to national renown, capturing the opportunities and inequalities of the Victorian age.

Available from www.lizshakespeare.co.uk

THE SONGS OF EDWARD CAPERN
Performed by
Nick Wyke and Becki Driscoll

The Songs of Edward Capern. A selection of poetry from the 19th Century Rural Postman Poet set to music by North Devon musicians Nick Wyke and Becki Driscoll. Inspired by the local folk music of the time, Wyke and Driscoll have carefully crafted their melodies and arrangements to enhance the character of the poems, and have included two of Edward Capern's own tunes, originally published in *"The Devonshire Melodist"* in the early 1860s.

   For more information please visit www.englishfiddle.com

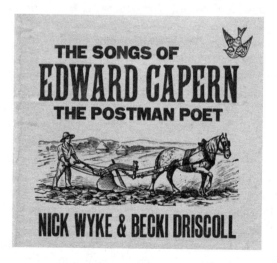

C.D. available from www.englishfiddle.com

ALL AROUND THE YEAR

Liz Shakespeare

These twelve poignant stories, deeply rooted in the Devon landscape, are each linked to a month of the year from January through to December. You will be transported from a sleepy village square to the wilds of Exmoor and from a summer beach to the narrow streets of a small Devon town, and introduced to a variety of memorable characters. In January, a young Croyde surfer tries to come to terms with her uncertain future. As signs of spring appear in the hedgerows, a farmer's wife starts a new venture. In August, a bereaved woman is deeply affected by an unexpected sight on Lynmouth beach. A Bideford man searches for a special Christmas present. All are at a moment of reckoning in their lives as they experience the subtle but significant events that make up everyday experience.

These stories of love and loss, of separation and reconciliation, will stay with you throughout the year.

"Sincere, emotional, touching; just three words that describe the stories in this book. Believable characters and the situations of everyday life which affect them are written in a moving and heart-warming way." *Devon Life*

"Liz Shakespeare's latest book is a collection of charming and compelling short stories rooted in the Devon landscape." *Exmoor Magazine*

"*All Around The Year* is a tribute to North Devon and to the people who live here." *Western Morning News.*

Available from www.lizshakespeare.co.uk

THE TURNING OF THE TIDE

Liz Shakespeare

Devon, 1871

Young and vulnerable Selina Burman from Clovelly and her two young children are confined in the harsh environment of Bideford Workhouse. She can only observe them from a distance and despairs of a better future. Her prospects improve when she meets Dr Ackland, a popular G.P. committed to social change. He employs her as a servant in his own household, despite the doubts of his wife and the Bideford community, for whom any connection with the Workhouse is a source of fear and shame. Selina's work gives satisfaction, but her search for love and security does not conform to the expectations of a middle class Victorian family and threatens to damage both her own future and Dr Ackland's career.

Set in Bideford and Clovelly, this novel draws on newspaper articles, letters and census returns, and powerfully brings to life the factual origins of the story.

'An immensely engaging story that captures the reader from the first page.' *Historical Novel Review*

'A clever combination of fact and fiction, this book both illuminates and entertains – an extremely gripping read.' *Family History Monthly*

'Liz Shakespeare understands the period perfectly well, describing the deprivation of the Union Workhouse as though she had suffered it herself.' *Devon Family Historian*

Available from www.lizshakespeare.co.uk

FEVER

A Story from a Devon Churchyard

Liz Shakespeare

How many of us have wandered through a country churchyard and been moved by the memorials to young children? In this book the author sets out to discover the truth behind a number of graves dating from just one year in a nineteenth century Devon village. Her compelling investigation reveals the harsh reality of life in a small village before the days of effective medical care. By skilfully weaving social history, research and imaginative reconstruction she builds a sympathetic portrait of a community in the midst of adversity.

We hear of strange remedies, the attempts of the clergy to help the stricken village, and the desperate poverty and over-crowding in farm labourers' cottages – the same cottages which are considered desirable today.

It is a story common to many rural communities; it is impossible to remain unmoved by the knowledge that this story is true.

'Fever is a good read, well-researched and dramatized with sensitivity.' *Western Morning News*

'A mixture of social history, research and imagination produces this sympathetic portrait of a community struggling to survive in harsh conditions... this book is a valuable reminder of how hard life used to be.' *Devon Life*

'This book gave me a great deal of pleasure to read. Liz Shakespeare has carried out her research very thoroughly.' *Devon Family Historian*

Available from www.lizshakespeare.co.uk

THE MEMORY BE GREEN
An Oral History of a Devon Village

Liz Shakespeare

When she first moved to Littleham near Bideford, Liz Shakespeare decided to capture a vanishing way of life by recording the memories of elderly men and women who were born early in the twentieth century. Farmers, housewives and labourers tell stories of oil lamps, outdoor privies, communal harvests, cattle drovers and the arrival of the first tractor. They describe in their own words the days when families kept a pig to supplement a simple diet and water had to be carried from the village pump.

In this remarkable book, the voices of a generation who are no longer with us reveal changes in village life which have been reflected throughout Devon and beyond.

'As generations die out and people's memories are lost to posterity, books like this with their invaluable eye-witness versions of village life in quieter times, form an important part of our literary heritage.' *North Devon Journal*

'People with modern 'romantic' views of pre-war rural life should read this book to obtain an insight into the reality of the experience.' *Western Morning News*

'It is a fine example of the value of oral testimony and how it can unlock memories stored away and ensure that the lives of ordinary people are not forgotten.' *Oral History*

Available from www.lizshakespeare.co.uk